MW01124998

Thinking in Algorithms

How to Combine Computer Analysis and
Human Creativity
for Better Problem-Solving and
Decision-Making

By Albert Rutherford

Copyright © 2021 by Albert Rutherford. All rights reserved.

No part of this publication may be reproduced, stored in a retrieval system, or transmitted in any form or by any means, electronic, mechanical, photocopying, recording, scanning or otherwise, except as permitted under Section 107 or 108 of the 1976 United States Copyright Act, without the prior written permission of the author.

Limit of Liability/ Disclaimer of Warranty: The author makes no representations or warranties with respect to the accuracy or completeness of the contents of this work and specifically disclaims all warranties, including without limitation warranties of fitness for a particular purpose. No warranty may be created or extended by sales or promotional materials. The advice and recipes contained herein may not be suitable for everyone. This work is sold with the understanding that the author is not engaged in rendering medical, legal or other professional advice or services. If professional assistance is required, the services of a competent professional person should be sought. The author shall not be liable for damages arising herefrom. The fact that an individual, organization of website is referred to in this work as a citation and/or potential source of further information does not mean that the author endorses the information the individual, organization to website may provide or recommendations they/it may make. Further, readers should be aware that Internet websites listed in this work might have changed or disappeared between when this work was written and when it is read.

For general information on the products and services or to obtain technical support, please contact the author.

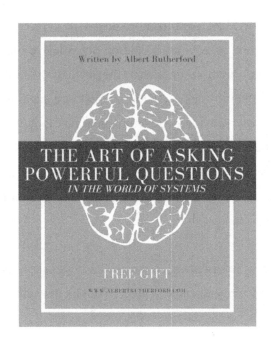

Visit www.albertrutherford.com and download your FREE GIFT: The Art of Asking Powerful Questions in the World of Systems

Table Of Contents

Table Of Contents _____ 7

Chapter 1: Homo Irrationalis _____ 9

Chapter 2: Machina Sapiens_____ 29

Chapter 3: Where Machines Teach Humans ___ 41

Chapter 4: Predictions, Dopamine, Machines, And
Humans_____ 59

Chapter 5: Diy Algorithm Design _____ 71

Chapter 6: The Procrastination Algorithm _____ 81

Chapter 7: The Overthinking Algorithm _____ 103

Conclusion _____ 125

Summary Guide _____ 127

Before You Go… _____ 133

References _____ 135

Endnotes _____ 137

Chapter 1: Homo Irrationalis

Humans are strange creatures. We often do things that don't make sense, sometimes even to ourselves. What makes us more willing to purchase a product for $4.99 than for $5.00? Why do we get items for 50% off that we would never buy at full price? And what makes us so eager to use products celebrities use when we have nothing in common?

Many of our decisions in life are seemingly random or based on whims. But even our most illogical actions are formulaic. As Dan Ariely says in his book *Predictably Irrational,* "these irrational behaviors of ours are neither random nor senseless. They are systematic, and since we repeat them again and again, predictable."[i]

Ariely is a psychology and behavioral economics professor at Duke University, a field of study that focuses on answering questions just like those we've posed. Researchers like Ariely have discovered the patterns behind our senseless habits by studying the effects of psychological, social, cognitive, and emotional factors on our economic decisions (Morgan, 2019).[ii] Behavioral economics not only teaches us about how our emotions, feelings, and biases affect our shopping but our entire lives.

The Truth About Our Gut feeling

We often talk about our "gut feeling" as this visceral, spur-of-the-moment urge to go in a certain direction or make a particular choice—an impulse towards doing what we feel is right. Similarly, we might tell someone to "listen to their heart" as a way of following their passions and desires, using their emotions to do what's best. Yet, we also tell people just as often to "use their head."

We think of using logic and using emotion to make decisions as separate ideas when they go hand-in-hand. As behavioral economics and psychology have discovered, it's next to impossible to decide without using our

10

feelings and biases. Our heads often defer to our hearts to help make quick choices.

Modern research and technology have looked into the brain and found it comprises a messy network of overlapping emotional and rational sections. Whether we like it or not, our rationality has been tainted by our feelings where the two are impossible to extricate. When comparing properties, making pros and cons lists may be the logical way of looking at things, but a feeling of home will usurp them every time. We may crunch the numbers to see if we can afford those new shoes we've been eyeing, but if we believe they'll bring us enough happiness, our minds will be made up no matter what our calculations say.

Even when we think we're making a logical choice, emotional impulses will seize control of situations and steer us in illogical directions. Our "gut" often hot-wires our decisions and takes them on a joyride to buy things for a rush of dopamine despite our empty wallets or to go on a date with an attractive person we know isn't good for us.

When we leap to conclusions and grab for the nearest solution or craving, we're not cutting out our brains completely. There's no way to be *that* carefree. Instead, our minds recognize that they must find a quick solution and speed up the process of decision-making to the degree that we might not even be able to follow. This isn't some miraculous hyper-speed thinking function but a simple process of shortcuts.

We've developed these shortcuts, known as "heuristics," as a survival mechanism that enables us to act more efficiently during a life-or-death situation. But, as we've evolved, it has become a less beneficial part of our everyday lives. Now we use quick thinking to make decisions about things that have no dire consequences or any consequences at all, like choosing whether we should get lettuce or spinach at the grocery store or picking out the next book we want to read from our shelf. Although heuristics speed up our thinking processes and work fine for inconsequential choices, they do so by creating corner-cutting habits that can be too simplistic for our own good.

Our Brains in Efficiency Mode

The more our society has grown and flourished, the more we have available to us—more entertainment, relationships, connectivity, knowledge...and more options. In fact, we have *too* many options. From the time we get up to the moment we fall asleep, we ask ourselves to decide on almost every minute of the day (sometimes more). But, for the most part, we don't notice these choices taking place. Our brains have gotten used to finding ways to function efficiently without interfering with the flow of our day. Like a server running in the background of a computer setup, our brains store, sort, process, and draw on information from previous experiences. This Rolodex of information allows our minds to be ready with conclusions to our questions before or quickly after they arise. This way, our day's flow isn't disturbed.

Our brains are like great warehouses of information. And when the boss (us) asks for a file, it's just too much work to run to the other end. Instead, the poor employee grabs for a nearer drawer. It might not have the exact or most correct answer the boss was looking for, but it's satisfactory enough that the job is considered finished. Maybe it's a B+ or a C+ type of answer, but it's good enough, and the employee is let off the hook.

Our brains don't just do this to make us happy; they do it to save energy. We only have so much brain power to give to decision making every day, so we have to make sure that we save it for the important stuff. There's no need to waste our fuel deciding what shoe goes on which foot or how to drive a car when we can put those actions on autopilot. If we gave our all to everything we had to choose in life, it would be like taking every possible road on how to work; we'd run out of gas long before we reached our destination.

We think of many of these skills and habits as naturally occurring instincts that we've always had. But that's not true. Once upon a time, we had to learn them. Some were intrinsic, like breathing, while others were difficult to discover and build, like riding a bike. But over time, they became second nature. We didn't need to think about them anymore. These processes that allow us to do our routine activities run in the background of our brain so we can focus on other things.

The more we can put skills on autopilot, the more complex ideas and complicated actions we can take on. When we save our energy on minor problems, we can put that extra fuel towards more important uses and questions, like figuring out the steps we need to take to further our career, deciding which relationships are worth holding onto or pondering our purpose and motivations in life.

Usually, this ability to save energy serves us well. It enables us to go about our daily activities with little effort or strain. But sometimes, the habit simplifies decision making too much. It leads us to make choices that aren't as logical as our brains might like us to believe.

Thanks to the research of behavioral economics, psychology, and neuroscience, we've come to understand many biases and shortcuts our brains use to make these leaps. And the better we understand them, the better we can combat them and move beyond them to more complex and rational forms of thinking.

Relative Advantage and Absolute Terms

When we make decisions, we often struggle to compare unlike or abstract things. Despite our irrational natures, our brains try their best to produce logical and critical thinking. They prefer concepts that can be nailed down, like comparing the cost of a $50 item to a $45 item or a score of 95% on a test versus a score of 86%. One is better (or cheaper) than the other. Their relativity to one another is clear and tangible. But choices in life are rarely so uncomplicated.

Imagine you're looking for a gift for your friend's wedding. You find the perfect item at a store nearby for around $50. It's more than you'd like to spend, but you decide that it's worth it because it's something you know they'll love. Before you get in the car, you remember that a similar store is having a sale one town over. You check and see that the item is in stock for $35. Would you go to the further store or the nearer store?

Chances are, you'd drive the few extra miles. The numerical values of $35 and $50 are easy to compare. One is cheaper than the other. But this considers only one variable: price. You haven't factored in the time spent driving or the gas needed to get there. These elements make the decision too complicated. From an easily comparable sum, the problem turns into a three-part formula, some aspects of which are abstract in value, such as the worth of your time.

We usually make choices about whether an item is "worth it" in one of two ways. When we see that a product has increased or decreased in value, such as by going on sale, and decide whether to buy it based on this, we are judging it based on "absolute terms." We are comparing it only with itself. However, this method is flawed. We have no true assessment of its worth except for the happenstance of its cost when we first encountered it. The product's value may be its sale price, its original price, or something else altogether. But we can't know that value for sure, so we base it off what information we have.

However, more often, we use another form of reasoning. When we compare an item to like items, such as a name brand and store brand, we are assessing its "relative advantage" by comparing it to similar or substitute products. When we get suckered into buying a "new and improved" version of something, we decide that the higher-priced version of the same item is of higher quality. If we choose the cheap knockoff, we assess the product's relative advantage in terms of cost and benefit. Although this suggests more data than absolute terms, it doesn't tell us the product's true value. But it does give context.

Our brain prefers and therefore seeks easier comparisons and calculations. We're more likely to buy something for $4.99 than $5.00. We're more ready to get something on sale. Numerical values make decisions easier to understand and explain. We can see the difference between two numbers, their relative value, and assess which one is 'better' based on our chosen comparison variable (i.e., price).

Sometimes using relative advantage will help us to see what's best in our spread of options. We won't know whether the first car we test drive is the best until we test a few others and see how they compare. But sellers and marketers can also take advantage of the way we compare rather than calculate. Take, for instance, a showroom with three cars. The salesperson walks you through the display to see the three options, which are all mid-size vehicles fit your needs. One is listed at

$30,000, another at $50,000, and the third at $80,000. Which do you go for?

Most of the time, the buyer will go for the middle option. The lower option seems too cheap compared to the other two, but $80,000 seems like it's too much to pay when you could get something similar for less. The salesperson knows this and will place a car they're looking to sell with two other options of lesser and higher values on purpose to make it seem like the best deal based on relative advantage (Ariely, p. 3).[iii]

Imprinting or the Anchoring Effect

Another issue we have with our reasoning is the undue importance we place on prior experiences. Too often, when we believe we're being logical and basing our choices on facts, we're just using our memories and biases to conclude.

Konrad Lorenz discovered this phenomenon while raising geese. When the goslings hatched, Lorenz realized that baby birds would attach themselves, or "imprint," on the closest figure available if the duck mother was absent. But this wasn't a temporary arrangement; it was an initial reaction that led to a permanent connection to the figure as a parent, no matter what it may be, Lorenz included.

We create similar relationships to products, using our first impressions and experiences with objects to deem their worth. In behavioral economics terms, this is called "anchoring" (Ariely, p. 28).[iv] If you see an item for the first time at $500 and, the next time, see that it's $400, you'll think the newer price must be a good deal. It doesn't matter whether the item's actual worth is $1,000 or $40.

This is also why you'll hear older generations bemoaning the cost of gas and milk prices. As inflation caused prices to rise, their perception of the worth of a product stayed the same. If they grew up with gas being $1 a gallon, its price would always seem high when it's over $1. One day, we'll also be saying things like, "back in my day, iPhones cost $1,000" because it's how the technology was introduced to us.

Herd Mentality

Society influences our decision making. Making choices because "everyone else is doing it" isn't the most logical. But when we see something is popular, we want to hop on the trend. Over 20,000 five-star reviews can't be wrong, and a long line of people can't be waiting around for nothing, right? And besides, it's much easier to go with the decision making of other people than it is to make choices for ourselves. This is called "herd mentality," and it's a troublesome phenomenon that has only become more difficult to avoid with social media and the internet.

Herding behavior can have great importance with stocks but is also an incredibly interesting part of human nature... and monkey nature. Michael Platt, a professor of neuroscience at the University of Pennsylvania, used cards with different shapes to study the decision making of monkeys. His team found that monkeys in the presence of other monkeys were more likely to choose the same option as the first monkey when presented with several cards than those who chose alone (Big Think, 2021).[v]

This is similar to the Asch conformity experiment of 1951, a test that asked participants to compare several lines to a target line and select the closest in length. However, the participants were placed in groups of people who were told to pick a particular wrong answer. The Asch experiment discovered that during several trials, the participants would become less sure of their own beliefs and start to choose the line everyone else was choosing (Mcleod, 2018).[vi]

Platt found that herd mentality relates to the social network of our brains, that part of our mind that recognizes the importance of others, leading us to analyze and mimic the actions of others (Big Think, 2021).[vii] Conforming is a type of survival mechanism. Standing out is more dangerous than giving up our individuality and fitting in. We're hardwired to avoid ostracization and prefer social acceptance.

Our Emotional Mind

Whether it's because of our emotions, past experiences, or other people's influence on us, our logical thinking often goes astray. But we can't blame our brains for being misled by our emotional impulses. It's the way they're wired to work.

Our emotions are the most straightforward and most accessible part of our brains to latch onto with decision making. Emotions are the first line of defense when a question arises. To make the best decisions would require going deeper into our mental capacities and using our more critical facilities. It would mean putting in much effort.

Emotional thinking comes to us naturally while rational decision making is learned. It requires intention and skill. Critical thinking only comes to us when we practice it repeatedly, making it a habit.

Emotions aren't the enemy, but they aren't reliable when used alone. We can take back control of our seemingly irrational behaviors by improving our rational thinking and questioning our decisions. Do I think about this logically or through the lens of past experiences? Why am I doing this? And what factors are guiding my hand?

To make sure that we're taking both aspects of thinking into account and start making rational thinking the norm rather than the exception, we can produce and use formulas for thinking and decision making to replace those we have that rely on biases and shortcuts.

Exercise

Take a day to reflect on your own decision making. Sit down and think about what choices you made on a given day, whether it was a decision to buy something, eat something, talk to someone, or some big life-altering choice. Then, think about these questions:

Do you feel regret about the choice you made or wish you could do it over?

What factors helped determine your choice, such as other people's opinions, price, previous experiences, etc.?

Now that you're warmed up, think about some bigger decision making you've done in the past and answer the questions below, whether in your head or on a piece of paper:

1. Take a moment to reflect on your own economic decision making by writing down your five biggest purchases in life and asking yourself these questions about each:

   a. Do you think they were worth it?

   b. Did they bring you the desired result, whether it was happiness, change, forward movement, etc.?

   c. What factors helped determine your choice? Did you compare it to other options to assess its value?

   d. Would you still buy the item today were you to have the option? Why or why not?

2. What are your five biggest regrets in life?
   a. Why do you regret those decisions?
   b. What made you make those decisions in the first place?
   c. Why did you believe they were a good idea?

3. What are five traits you dislike about yourself (e.g., stubbornness, procrastination, etc.)?
   a. Why do you dislike these traits?

Chapter 2: Machina Sapiens

In our world of modern technology, many decisions we make are weighed heavily by the algorithms of machines, although we may not always know it. Whenever we Google a question, scroll through social media or click on an ad, we're setting off complex calculations.

Take, for instance, a simple search for a car repair service. You type into the Google search bar "car repair service" and get the answer you need in a few seconds. But in those seconds, numerous formulas are running. Google uses specific algorithms to select pages from millions of options to find the most helpful you, considering your location and your previous inquiries about cars and car repairs. It factors in similar pages you've looked at before and which ones you've liked and clicked on or not liked and quickly exited out of or scrolled past. Depending on what you've searched before,

Google may even have a good idea of what car you have and recommend car repair services specifically for those vehicles. The search engine weighs all these elements based on importance and relevance while also using its standards to assess the page itself. The algorithm looks through text and images to see if the selections are 'good' sites or not, meaning that they're comprehensive and match applicable search terms. And it does all this in the blink of an eye.

We don't think about how complicated this underground search process is when we type our question. We're just happy to find a result that will help us get our car fixed. But if we consider how much headache and time it can shave off, Google's search engine is an incredible invention. Of course, a lot of this digital digging is a marketing tactic used by companies and Google itself to show us ads and other sources of revenue. But a large part of it is also to better display the worlds of knowledge at our fingertips in a digestible way and make decision making easier for us. Sometimes, our technology even tries to provide us with solutions *before* we ask questions.

Have you ever been scrolling through Facebook or Instagram and stumbled on an ad for something that seems just perfect for you? And you wonder: 'How did it know?' It may seem like a coincidence, but it's precise algorithms using your data. These sites take your information, such as your location, age, gender, likes and dislikes, and search history, to understand your habits and predict what products you like or need. And, usually, they do a good job.

Machine Learning

Algorithms are always learning and evolving based on the information we give them. The more we search and use them, the better they become at knowing what we like and want. Just like humans, they pick up on cues and fix mistakes to do things better each time. This is called machine learning.

Often, machine learning is lumped with AI algorithms. Although they're often used together, they're not the same. An algorithm decides what to show you or produce, while machine learning is a subfield of AI that tracks your online presence and interactions to understand your tendencies and habits. AI algorithms are the more logical, process-driven side of technology, like the directions for baking a cake. Meanwhile, machine learning is the more abstract component, the human-like factor dipping its finger into the batter to see whether it's sweet enough. The two parts must work together to find success; algorithms have to learn to know a change must be made, and machine learning has to have an algorithm to solve issues that arise.

Although algorithms are powerful and at the core of many technologies we lean on today, machine learning has quickly become more influential. Yet, machine learning is based on human nature. People don't just rely on what they learn initially but grow and evolve to better understand themselves and the world around them. Machine learning imitates this through a more scientific method that generates and tests new ideas to see the viability of hypotheses. With the power of technology and AI, machine learning is usually much faster at this process than we are.

AI Algorithms and Advertising

Good marketers have tapped into the potential of both AI algorithms and machine learning. And it's almost scary how accurate it can be. But humans are more predictable than we might think.

In many ways, marketers and machine learning have made our lives much easier. The algorithms advertisers use to sell us products and services help narrow down the millions of options available to us. But they can also be misconstrued and are often used in ways we don't fully understand or for purposes we don't like.

To make social media more desirable and fun (i.e., addictive), algorithms are put in place to keep you invested by learning what you like and dislike and showing you only information you enjoy interacting with. On the surface, this helps weed out uninspired or annoying posts you don't want to see and helps to make the scope of what you're looking at more manageable. But this also narrows your field of vision. Often, you'll find you have posts only from certain people in your feed, usually those that already agree with you on topics, and never see what differing points of view have to say.

These echo chambers may feel comforting, but they create a false sense of security in which we're led to believe more people agree with us than do. It's easy to feel like the majority when all you hear are your thoughts bouncing back at you. But the more we become surrounded by "yes men" who agree with us, the less we'll be able to practice healthy debate. When we never run into opposition, we don't know how to handle it when it arises and are more likely to pretend it doesn't exist.

This filtering can be even more dangerous in other sectors, such as Google News, which uses your search history and interactions to gauge what stories you want to see. Such algorithms don't consider what information you *should* be seeing or *need* to be seeing but what you most enjoy. So, if you always click on videos of cute cats and never want to read about politics or foreign trade, you'll be very informed about kittens and not very informed about world issues.

Having a curated feed may make us happy and sometimes be helpful, but remember that the main goal of these algorithms is self-serving. Their primary aim is to keep us using the apps and programs they're designed for. Google News wants you to stay informed, but only through *their* application. Therefore, it prioritizes ads and engagement over learning and knowledge.

It's nearly impossible to escape these algorithms and the ulterior motives that often go along with them. But we can understand them. And, by doing so, use them for our benefit.

What is an Algorithm, Anyways?

Not all machine learning and AI technologies are used for advertising. Algorithms are everywhere: from code on websites to the sensors in your car, your bank account, and the stoplight on the street. Some algorithms are simple, calculating the time since the last light and the status of the other lights around them. Others are more complicated, running millions of data points in moments to create a result. Yet even the most complex processes follow the same set of simple parameters.

When you break it down into its most basic parts, an algorithm is merely a sequence of steps to perform a task given an initial situation (Fisher, p. 4).[viii] These sequences will be long and elaborate, like the millions of data points running simultaneously to create a Google search result. Others will be so basic that they might not even be mathematical.

Recipes, directions, and sewing patterns are all forms of algorithms too.

We need not be coders or mathematicians to think about algorithms, use them, or even create our own. At their core, good algorithms have four simple characteristics:

> **Correct:** The answer comes from previous knowledge and calculations and follows logic.
>
> **Efficient:** The algorithm must use only the space and time necessary to get the best result.
>
> **Comprehensible:** The algorithm can be understood by others.
>
> **Illustrative:** The solution can be applied to create greater concepts, such as by sorting data. (Fisher, p. 7)[ix]

When we see algorithms in a more simplistic way, we can use them to help us sort concepts and ideas into actionable steps.

Our Minds as Machines

AI algorithms and machine learning may be more rational and logical (plus more efficient) than humans can ever hope to be. But we have something machines and AI don't. The human mind is a powerful place...perhaps not when it comes to quickly solving formulas, but with emotion, abstraction, and imagination.

Our minds work in much broader and more interesting ways than machine learning and AI can. Those systems know only input and output. They know how to move from A to B. But we understand, intrinsically, a lot more about abstract ideas.

The same traits that weigh down our critical thinking can also be some of our greatest strengths. Although we may look at our rational side in high esteem, our irrational decision making has its importance too. Sure, it may be illogical to choose what city to move to based on the *feeling*. But being happy where you live is crucial. Maybe it seems silly to buy a pair of shoes just because they put a smile on your face, but why shouldn't you surround yourself with things that make you grin? These are concepts that AI and machine learning do not fully understand.

We may see the problems and solutions AI deals with as too complex for our simple minds, but if they could, they would probably say the same about many decisions we have to make. As Christian and Griffiths point out in their book *Algorithms to Live By*, "Life is full of problems that are, quite simply, hard. And the mistakes made by people often say more about the intrinsic difficulties of the problem than about the fallibility of human brains" (p. 5).[x]

This is exactly why we need as many tools in our toolkit as we can get. If we put the rational side of algorithms *and* our abilities of imagination and abstraction together, we can achieve incredible things. When we use the abilities of algorithms to our advantage, we can become more efficient and rational decision makers. We can make choices with more surety and have fewer regrets. We can move forward more effectively and spend our time more wisely.

Exercise

Test the powers of machine learning and AI algorithms in your life by switching up your routine. For example, search for something you would never normally search for or look at and interact with the profile of someone you never engage with on social media.

Watch, in these few days, how the algorithms change their approach to your content. Did you see an ad you've never seen before? Did you see posts you'd never normally have on your feed? How did this affect your life or mood?

Chapter 3: Where Machines Teach Humans

When you look at the world through algorithms, it may seem like it would get a lot more complex, but it actually becomes much simpler. As humans, we often overthink things with our emotions and past experiences. We see every decision as its own solitary issue with a unique set of difficulties and rewards. But, mathematically speaking, many of these problems come down to the same fundamentals.

Think back to your high school math class; when combined and utilized correctly, the same set of formulas were used for a myriad of problems. The most complicated equations came down to the same root functions: addition, subtraction, multiplication, and division. When faced with a new algebraic problem, the solution didn't require inventing new ways of adding and subtracting but simply picking the right form of calculation, inputting the values, and solving for X. The same goes for applying algorithms to our everyday lives.

When you look past the emotional ties and biases attached to most choices in life, you'll see how similar many are. For instance, finding a parking spot, hiring a new assistant, buying a house, and choosing a romantic partner seem like very separate dilemmas. Yet, they can all be solved with one equation: "optimal stopping."

"Optimal Stopping"[xi]

Imagine you've just ended a relationship and have jumped back into the dating world. Ending a date with someone who finally shares your interests, you wonder: Is this as good as it gets? Your friends tell you there are more fish in the sea. But you've seen enough duds to know many of those fish are best left off the hook. With every bad date, you feel the clock ticking down towards desperation. Every day you wait to text back the ones you liked heightens the risk they'll find someone else.

So, do you keep looking? Or settle down with the best so far?

Christian and Griffiths have given us the research to answer this lifelong dilemma. The optimal time to stop shopping around and choose from your current spread of options, whether you're looking at products on a retail shelf or life partners, is when you've seen 37% of the merchandise. This number is the tipping point between having seen enough of what's out there to make an informed decision and passing by so many options you limit yourself. After 37%, the likelihood that you've already found the best option and passed it by becomes too high.

The 37% rule was first coined the "secretary problem" as it gained popularity as a riddle in a 1960s issue of *Scientific American* about choosing the best secretary for an open position (Christian & Griffiths, p. 10).[xii] Since then, mathematicians have seen the idea's potential behind the puzzle and researched and written numerous papers on its importance and possible uses, which have turned out to be nearly limitless.

Imagine you're so fed up with dating that you take drastic measures and sign up for a dating show, hoping it will pressure you to make a choice. Either you'll pick one of the three options or walk away with nothing. The only catch is that you must interview each Romeo candidate independently and choose yes or no on the spot before moving on to the next. Say no to the first two, and you'll be stuck with the third. Say yes to the first, and you'll never even meet the other two. So, what do you do? This simplifies the secretary problem, which demonstrates the risk you take when moving forward and the risk you take with making a choice too early. Although the stakes are high, the solution is easy when you think of the problem from a mathematical viewpoint.

Suitor #1 will automatically be the best yet. But there's nothing to compare them to. Perhaps it will get better. Or perhaps it won't. Because you have no data, choosing #1 is no better than random selection. Suitor #1 has a

100% chance of being the best if they're the only option. But once Suitor #2 is introduced, Suitor #1's chances will drop to 50%. Suitor #2's chances are also 50%. However, their arrival to the problem brings the advantage of comparison. Although you can no longer choose Suitor #1, they have provided you with a baseline to decipher the quality of Suitor #2. By the time the third and final suitor is introduced, the chance of any of the three is a good fit goes down to 33%. You now know the full spread of options, but only one is still available to you, and their likelihood of being the best has only grown smaller.

Therefore, picking the second option is your best bet. Why? When you meet only one out of three choices, you lack information. But once you get to the third, you lose your freedom of choice; there's only one option left. Whether you like it or not, you're stuck with it. The other two candidates have been asked to leave the set.

The second Romeo gives you both information and freedom. If they're worse than #1, you can dismiss them and still have a 50% chance for success with Romeo #3. If they're better than #1, it's smart to settle. You, again, have a 50% chance of choosing well. You have the right combination of data and agency by going just far to see your choices but not as far as to tire them out. And that is the compromise of the 37% rule.

The same optimal stopping rules apply whether you have three candidates or 1,000 (Christian & Griffiths, p. 14).[xiii] You can see from the table below that when dealing with three candidates, the best time to "leap" is after one. With five people, it is best to choose after two, and so on.

Number of Dates	Settle Down After	Chances of Having a Good Match
3	1 (33.33%)	50%
5	2 (40%)	43.33%
10	3 (30%)	39.87%
20	7 (35%)	38.42%

50	18 (36%)	37.43%
100	37 (37%)	37.10%
1000	369 (36.9%)	36.81%

You may be wondering... but what if the second date out of the three is the worst? That could very well happen. The secretary problem isn't a surefire way of ending up with a perfect match or a perfect answer, but it is the best way to choose efficiently. And, as we saw above, if the second date is worse than the first, we still have a 50% chance for success with #3. The more options you give yourself, the less likely, statistically, that you'll be to pick the best one. Going on just one date means you'll always choose the best one because it's the only one, while going on 50 dates will leave you with a diminished chance of walking away successfully. However, if you use the optimal stopping algorithm, your chances will always be somewhere around 37%.

Look-then-Leap Rule

Optimal stopping is more helpful for realistic situations when applied to look-then-leap thinking. The first part of this process is the "looking" phase in which you window shop, exploring your options and gathering data with a strict promise not to buy. After the designated time for research runs out, you "leap" and commit to picking the first option that outshines everyone seen so far (Christian & Griffiths, p. 13).[xiv]

Imagine you're staying at a rental house on vacation with friends. You get the first pick of the bedrooms, but your friends are close behind. Pass one by, and it'll get snatched up. If applying the 37% rule to a five-bedroom home, you'll pass by the first bedroom no matter what it looks like—even if it has a king-size bed and a ginormous television. Optimal stopping alone would suggest you pick the second bedroom, but if you find that bunk beds, a flickering light, and a broken heater await you, the look-then-leap rule allows you to move past. From there, you'll carry on until you either exhaust all choices or find something better than what you've seen thus far, such as a master suite with a jacuzzi, California king, and access to the pool.

The larger your number of options, the better the look-then-leap rule works, as you'll have more information. A five-bedroom home will only allow you a sample size of two rooms before you must start making choices, while a ten-bedroom mansion will give you three bedrooms to base your decision on.

Optimal stopping and the look-then-leap rule can be applied not just to dating and bedrooms, but almost anything, such as going on job interviews, buying a house, or even looking at colleges. The ideas and the emotions surrounding each situation are quite different, but by looking at the problem mathematically, you'll find they're all simple calculations.

However, the secretary problem only applies to situations where we have little to no data, or what mathematicians call "no-information games" (Christian & Griffiths, p. 20).[xv] While we're sometimes forced to make such uninformed decisions, we often have more opportunities to educate ourselves.

If, for instance, instead of dating just any Joe Schmoe you meet, you use a dating service that asks applicants to fill out a detailed form that calculates whether you'll be a good match or not and spits out a score, optimal stopping no longer applies. You have another type of more concrete and comparable data to use in making your choice. Don't worry, there's an algorithm for this as well: the "threshold rule."

"The Threshold Rule"[xvi]

If we lived in the realm of strict numerical values, choosing who to select as a partner, who to hire for a job opening, or even what college to go to would become obvious: Just pick the one with the highest score. Sometimes, this is possible in the real world, but we'll often run into a similar issue as that of optimal stopping.

Let's say we can measure the compatibility between two people using a questionnaire. If the first date you go on has a score of 98 out of 100, that's a clear choice. But what if it was 50? The odds that the next choice will have a higher score are hit-or-miss. Do you continue dating and risk that everyone afterward will score lower or stick with what you've got?

The threshold rule is similar to optimal stopping because it helps us decide when to stop looking for a candidate or to make a decision. But while optimal stopping is about ensuring data is gathered, the threshold rule is about leveraging the information we *already have* as efficiently as possible. The threshold rule teaches us that the more options we have left, the less likely it is that our current selection is the best one out there, and the more seriously we must consider whether our standards are low enough.

Let's say the dating show you're on requires that contestants take a compatibility quiz. The first suitor has a score of 40% out of 100%. Since that's less than 50%, the chances the next suitor will be higher are good, and you pass. Then, if Suitor #2 tells you they have a score of 50%, the odds that the last candidate will be higher are 50/50. Whereas optimal stopping would tell you to stick with this second choice, including new data makes this a different situation. You now know what would be needed for Suitor #3 to be better than Suitor #2 and what they probably will be. And, since it's equally likely they'll be worse or better, the threshold rule states you should take the chance and pick the last option.

From deciding whether an item is cheap enough to buy to whether you should take that job with a low salary or wait for something better, the threshold rule is a helpful tool for many situations. But, most notably, it has been used to evaluate offers when selling a house.

Christian and Griffiths use this example to illustrate the threshold rule in *Algorithms to Live By*. Using offers between $400,000 and $500,000, the optimal offer can be calculated based on the cost per offer, whether that be a decrease in the offers themselves, an advertising fee, or the cost of the mortgage and utilities you must pay to remain in the house. If the cost per offer is $2,000, the optimal offer would be $480,000 or more. A cost of $10,000 per offer would suggest you should take anything at or above $455,279 (Christian & Griffiths, p. 21-22).[xvii]

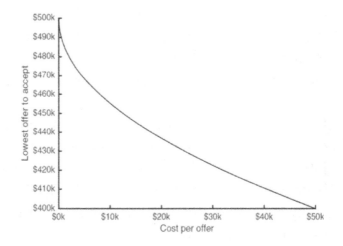

Optimal stopping thresholds in the house-selling problem.

You never know what will happen by just going with your gut on an offer and hoping for the best. But, by following the threshold rule, you can make a much more informed decision and have less regret by knowing what's likely to occur afterward and whether it's better than your current option.

Knowing When to Quit: The Burglar Problem

Some decisions aren't based on when to jump into a scenario, like buying a house, but when to get out. Optimal stopping works for this too when reshaped into "the burglar problem." In this scenario, a burglar goes on a robbery spree. The more robberies the burglar takes on, the more money he'll make. However, more robberies also mean more opportunities for being discovered, increasing risk. So, when should he stop? The calculation is simple: you have only to divide the chances the robber will get away by the chance of getting caught (Christian & Griffiths, p. 27).[xviii]

Let's say you're on a trivia game show. Every round has four questions, and the categories get steadily more difficult. If all the questions are simple math and you're very good at math, the likelihood of answering each question right might be around 95%. That makes the likelihood you'll make an error and choose the wrong answer 5%. By dividing your chances of getting the right answer and doubling your winnings (95) by the chances of making a mistake and walking away with nothing (5) you'll know you should quit after 19 rounds (95/5=19). However, if the questions were about something you know nothing about, such as animals from the Mariana Trench, which creates a very different situation. If you make a random guess on the questions, you'll have a 25% chance of getting it right and a 75% chance of getting it wrong. This game is much riskier. You should quit after only one round (25/75= 0.33) *if* you even get that far.[xix]

The Problem with Optimal Stopping

Optimal stopping in its many forms has been proven to work, yet, people are too impatient to use it. A 1990 study by Amnon Rapoport and Darryl Seale repeated numerous iterations of the secretary problem for applicants and found that participants choose too early 80% of the time. But only marginally. Participants usually chose a candidate who was almost, but not quite, optimal (Christian & Griffiths, p. 28-29). [xx]

In real life, the secretary problem has stakes beyond losing a perfect candidate, it also takes up our time, which we value highly. Perhaps even more than getting the best result. In an imaginary scenario, time is no factor. Yet, participants acted as if it was. Rapoport and Seale found that participants were correct in choosing when they did (Christian & Griffiths, p. 29).[xxi] The respondents hadn't thought about this consciously but taken time into account intrinsically.

Even when we don't realize it, humans value time above most things. We're aware of its passing and its cost, which may be why we're so fixated on getting things done quickly.

Exercise

Apply optimal stopping or one of its derivatives to a decision you've made in your own life, whether it be selling a house, taking a job offer, picking a partner, or just buying an item at the grocery store. Then, consider:

1. Did you choose at the optimal time or price?

2. If not, what factors did you use to decide when to stop?

3. Had you used optimal stopping, would you have ended up with the same result or something different?

4. If it would have been different, would this have been a better or worse choice?

Chapter 4: Predictions, Dopamine, Machines, and Humans

In Kuwait in February of 1991, Commander Lieutenant Michael Riley faced the choice that no one likes to encounter in life: an impossible one. While monitoring radar screens, Riley noticed an incoming blip that made his blood turn cold. He had a feeling that the marker was a missile, which seemed headed straight for one of the ships in port. But he had no logical evidence to support his gut reaction. Riley had seen many similar blips during his shift, which were usually harmless fighter jets who had turned off their communications to avoid detection by the Iraqis. The blips looked the same either way. The only way to distinguish between a deadly missile and a harmless jet was their altitude, which could not be read by the radar he had.

If the blip were a missile, the fleet would be destroyed, and numerous lives would be lost. But if it was a fighter jet, Riley would have authorized friendly fire and would lose his job. He decided to go with his gut and fire.

Hours later, when a team finally went and viewed the wreckage, they found the remains of a Silkworm missile. Riley had been right. But no one, including himself, knew why. Hours upon hours of analysis by experts revealed there was no way Riley could have distinguished the blip.

At least, until 1993, when Gary Klein, who had been studying decision making in high-intensity situations, investigated Riley's case from a psychological viewpoint.
Eventually, he found the answer; although the radar Riley used could not show altitude, the lieutenant had evaluated it subconsciously due to the timing of when the blip appeared. The missile was initially masked by ground interference, making it appear later than if it had been a fighter jet flying in from above (Lehrer, 28-34). [xxii]

Riley, nor any of his colleagues, had realized this. Riley had not understood what he had based his decision making on and thought he had only gotten lucky. When, in reality, he had learned a crucial skill he hadn't even been aware of. His brain had predicted the outcome of the scenario without him knowing.

Dopamine

The chemical that allowed Riley to decide was dopamine. Most people know dopamine as the brain's happy chemical, but it does a lot more than put us in a good mood. Dopamine is the communicator neuron, the SMS of brain cells.

In the 1970s, a medical student named Wolfram Schultz discovered dopamine was a reward chemical while studying monkeys. He found that dopamine was released when good things happened to the primates, like receiving a tasty treat. But Schultz's studies showed that the chemical was also released when good things were merely *predicted* to occur. For example, if a tone was sounded before feeding time, the monkeys would come to associate the auditory trigger with the reward. Thus, their brains would release dopamine when they heard the sound, even if no food was given (Lehrer, 36-37).[xxiii] Our brains do the same. For instance, we feel joy from shopping online for new clothes or electronics although we can't yet wear or use them.

Schultz's study proved that dopamine was more concerned with predicting good results than actually receiving rewards, and the chemicals were seen anew as "prediction neurons." When predictions were right, such as food following a tone associated with feeding, dopamine was released. But if predictions were wrong, and no reward was given when it was expected to be, dopamine decreased (Lehrer, 36-37).[xxiv]

When errors are made in predicting, the brain sends a signal from the anterior cingulate cortex (ACC) known as "error-related negativity." The ACC oversees learning from the predictions of dopamine, keeping track of how often our assumptions are right and how often they're wrong to do better next time. When we're wrong, the error report signal goes to the thalamus, which is in charge of conscious attention, and the hypothalamus is responsible for subconscious bodily function (Lehrer, 38-39).[xxv] These sections of the brain are nearly complete opposites and affect our decision making in different ways. When our hypothalamus enters the conversation, we might feel sweaty or have that gut-wrenching feeling we associate with bad situations. Meanwhile, the thalamus produces logical and critical thinking.

The Truth About our Gut Feeling

Just as Riley found in his life-threatening situation, the signal to the hypothalamus is often faster than that to our thalamus, causing us to have bodily reactions before our thoughts can catch up. Scientists created a test to observe this phenomenon with a simple game where a dealer drew one card each from four decks and placed them face down on a table. Participants would then choose one of the cards, which would say whether or not the player won and how much money they had earned or owed. The trick was that two of the decks were better than the others; one had higher payouts and bigger risks while the other had consistent yet smaller payouts and rarely asked players to pay.

After only 10 cards, players began to have bodily reactions to the bad decks, such as anxiousness, sweating, and nervousness. Yet, it took over 30 draws to learn from this reaction and 50 to realize what was actually happening. Meanwhile, those who had trouble experiencing emotions due to neurological impairments never had a gut reaction to the cards. They never learned that the game was rigged and eventually went into debt. Their lack of emotional awareness had prevented them from making better choices (Lehrer, p. 46-47).[xxvi]

Our brains stop firing dopamine when our predictions are wrong and fire more when our predictions are right, teaching us the difference between good and bad choices by rewarding us with pleasurable feelings. We use this to learn several skills, such as playing a good game of chess.

When the Mind is better than the Machine

In 1997, the world was humbled by what they referred to as "a glorified calculator," a computer called Deep Blue that used mathematics to beat the greatest chess player in the world: Garry Kasparov (Wilson et al.). While a mere mortal like Kasparov could only calculate around five moves per second, Blue could assess an incredible two-hundred million, allowing it to understand nearly every possible outcome. However, to process that many predictions in such a small time frame took much energy. So much that Deep Blue was a fire hazard. Meanwhile, Kasparov's brain used less energy than a single light bulb (Lehrer, p. 43).[xxvii]

Despite losing the match, the efficiency of Kasparov's brain awed Gerald Tesauro, the original mastermind behind Deep Blue, and inspired him to create a more human-like machine. He came up with TD-Gammon, a backgammon playing computer that used "temporal difference." TD started with no knowledge of the game and played itself repeatedly until it *learned* how to be better (Lehrer, p. 44).[xxviii] While Deep Blue was an incredibly smart and powerful machine, its abilities paled compared to the efficiency of the simplified TD-Gammon version. Yet TD-Gammon made many mistakes until it learned from them, just like a human.

Emotions, Evidence, and Bayesian Analysis

Studies have shown that both amateur players and grandmasters considered only four or five possible moves on any turn. Yet, a grandmaster who was much better at deciphering those four to five moves would create the best outcome (Wilson et al.). After playing hundreds if not thousands of games, humans learned which options out of the nearly infinite moves were most likely to occur and where they would lead. Meanwhile, their dopamine receptors encouraged their wins and correct choices with pleasure.

Before we or a machine like TD-Gammon understand how to play chess well, all options are equally likely to create the desired effect.

This is called "prior probability," because it's the information we have before knowing anything about the situation (Domingos, p. 146).[xxix] If we play one game where we move our queen first and end up losing, we might have some inkling that this move is a bad choice. But it could also be a fluke. If we lose every game where we play our queen first, we'll *learn* that this is a bad choice and stop making the mistake of trying those strategies where we found success or saw others have success. This is called "posterior probability" because it relies on gathered evidence (Domingos, p. 146).[xxx]

Our bodies and brains already use the basic ideas behind prior probability and posterior probability abstractly, but we can also use an algorithm, called Bayesian analysis, to predict outcomes more concretely. Bayesian analysis relies on the principles of Bayes' theorem, which simply suggests that we should use any evidence we gain to update and verify our hypothesis. This algorithm uses the basic principle of cause and effect and the power of mathematics to assess the probability of an event given the situation and prior outcomes (Domingos, p. 144-145).[xxxi]

The rules of the card game mentioned were simplified so red cards (hearts and diamonds) lost and black cards (spades and clubs) lost. Without even playing a single round, our likelihood of drawing red is 50%, and our likelihood of drawing black is 50%. That's our prior probability because we have only the situation and no evidence. But, if we begin to draw cards and find that seven out of our first ten draws were black, we must acknowledge that our chances are skewed. Our new evidence, or posterior probability, shows we have a 70% chance of pulling a black card and a 30% chance of pulling a red card.

If the likelihood of winning and drawing a red card is still 50% would be an incomplete analysis given this new information, but ignoring statistics altogether in favor of our experiences is too biased. Bayesian analysis allows us to combine these two factors into one calculation:
$$P(D)=P(D|H)P(H)+P(D|H)P(H)$$

In this equation, P stands for probability, H stands for hypothesis, and D stands for data. Here, our hypothesis is that we'll draw a red card and win. And our data is the likelihood of this effect occurring given our evidence.

When you multiply the probability of a red

card (50%) by the likelihood of getting a red card based on evidence (30%), you come up with a 15% chance of drawing red. However, you must also consider the unlikelihood. There is a 50% you will draw a black card based on statistics and a 70% chance of drawing black based on evidence, which amounts to a 35% chance of losing. When combined, you'll find your chance of winning is 5%.[xxxii]

Unlike the usual calculations of probability, or the "frequentist" interpretation, Bayesian analysis uses an interpretation of probability that emphasizes using an effect or outcome to find the cause rather than the other way around (Domingos, p. 148-149).[xxxiii] Whereas frequentists use the simple measure of discovering how often a certain event occurs given as many tests as possible, Bayesian analysis is more useful for open-ended ideas and observation, such as those intuitions we naturally use in our day-to-day life to make decisions. It considers not only mathematical statistics but real-life tendencies and biases that occur, which is more suitable for the irrational way humans naturally predict future events.

When we hone our intuition abilities, listening to where our dopamine steers us, and questioning why it is doing so, we can start to understand the logic behind our gut reaction. Compared with mathematics like Bayesian analysis, this can be a powerful tool for looking at the possibilities that await us, making us better and more efficient at scheduling our time, but only if we can overcome our tendencies to procrastinate and overthink.

The next three chapters will show how to design our own algorithms to live a better life. First, I will talk about the algorithm design process and then walk you through two examples of how to apply it to overcome two bad habits, procrastination and overthinking.

Chapter 5: DIY Algorithm Design

Houston, we have a problem!

Alright, how do we solve it?

Our lives are peppered with problems; small ones, big ones, and seemingly insurmountable ones. But no matter how big or small our troubles are, their solution always starts with a plan. In this book, we call that plan an algorithm.

So far, we have learned that our decision-making process is not as reliable as we'd like to think. We are emotional, not rational actors. We also learned that computers do a good job at replicating optimized solutions to specific problems. However, with abstract thinking, computers can't make good calls.

In this chapter and the following two, we will finally bring together all that we learned to merge the best of artificial and human intelligence. We will use an algorithmic formula to design optimal solutions to abstract problems, such as overcoming procrastination and nib overthinking in the bud.

I'm about to present the formula I designed by Stephen Edwards, Brian Dorn, and Dean Sanders on their website, Objects First.[xxxiv] There are many types of algorithms. Your grandma's pumpkin pie recipe is an algorithm. How to connect your wireless headphones to your phone is an algorithm. A map about how to get from A to B is an algorithm. And so is the Pythagorean theorem. Some algorithms are formal-mathematical, others graphical, or informal. Therefore, we can create our algorithm in multiple ways, too. If the algorithm solves our problem, the form doesn't matter too much.

Objects First's algorithm plan highlights five key steps we will also use here.

"Step 1: Obtain a description of the problem.

Step 2: Analyze the problem.

Step 3: Develop a base algorithm.

Step 4: Refine the algorithm by adding more detail.

Step 5: Review the algorithm."[xxxv]

This five-step sequence is not our algorithm, and this is our plan to generate the algorithm. In Steps 1 and 2, we will explore the problem we want to solve and collect data. We need to understand where we are right now and where we want to go (a.k.a. our solution). Based on this knowledge, we will create our base, or base algorithm in Step 3. In Step 4, we can add more details to the base algorithm, if we find it helps us get to our solution quicker. Step 5 will be about reviewing and testing our algorithm. We need to make sure that it works reliably every single time. If it doesn't produce consistent results, we may need to add, subtract, or tweak some of its elements. In the review process, you can also assess if the algorithm generally applies to problems of that nature or if it only works in a specific case. For example, does it work on any procrastination or does it work only with work-related procrastination?

Let's break down each step and see what they mean.

Step 1: Obtain a description of the problem.

When we're considering computer algorithms, there is a client – the person with a problem. And we have a developer who helps the client solve the problem, creating an algorithm. The client needs to describe their issue as objectively, clearly, and completely as possible. And then, the developer's task is to be sensitive to any biases, assumptions, incomplete, or contradictory information in the client's retelling and design the algorithm considering the above. In the process we're working on, you are both the client and the developer.

Your task, thus, is to first define the problem and possible, respecting the parameters mentioned above. Then revise your words, checking for inconsistencies, biases, and assumptions. You can ask other people's opinions if you fear you might have blind spots even after the revision.

Step 2: Analyze the problem.

In this step, we want to cement points A and B. A is our starting point, where we are now. And B is the optimal solution, where we want to arrive.

To define our starting point, we need to answer these questions:

- "What data are available?
- Where is that data?
- What formulas pertain to the problem?
- What rules exist for working with the data?
- What relationships exist among the data values?"[xxxvi]

When designing the end point, we need to be as precise describing the desired solution as possible. We need to know exactly where we're headed and how it will look and feel when we're there. We must know the full address we're headed to before inserting it in our GPS. How could we get to our destination otherwise? These questions can help you in this endeavor:

- "What new facts will we have?
- What items will have changed?
- What changes will have been made to those items?
- What things will no longer exist?"[xxxvii]

Step 3: Develop a base algorithm.

Time to get creative and proactive. Sketch a rough sequence of steps you could start with to get from A to B based on all the data. The creators of Objects First highly recommend starting with a base algorithm "that includes the major part of a solution, but leaves the details until later."

A base algorithm need not be complicated. Here is an example of a base algorithm. *I want to drink hot chocolate, but I don't have milk.* The algorithm:

- Go to the supermarket.

- Select the preferred type of milk.

- Purchase the milk.

- Boil the milk.

- Add cocoa powder.

- Drink the hot chocolate.

It is simple, efficient, replicable, and consistent. It's guaranteed that if you repeat this sequence of events each time you want to drink hot chocolate but you don't have milk, you'll get the same result. Sure, your milk may be out of stock at the supermarket. What can you do then? Here is where Step 4 comes in.

Step 4: Refine the algorithm by adding more detail.

Now that we have the base algorithm, we can get deeper into optimization by adding details. How much detail are we talking about? It's situation dependent. We need to consider multiple factors, such as whether we can consistently execute the algorithm with the extra steps. Do we know how to do it? For example, do we know how much cocoa should we add to our milk? Or if we asked someone to buy the milk for us, would they know which milk to choose? Or if the store was out of our preferred milk, would we be willing to buy another milk, or we'd just abort the hot chocolate mission?

Here you have the chance to add more specific instructions and generate alternatives if some steps don't work out.

Step 5: Review the algorithm.

The last thing we need to do is a review, test, take notes, and tweak the algorithm. The most important part of this process is to see if the algorithm solves our problem. If it doesn't, we need to add details or change aspects of the base algorithm until we get the desired results. Once the algorithm solves our problem, it's recommended to run the following follow-up questions:

- Is this solution adoptable to only a specific problem or could it be generalized?
- Could this solution be simplified?

You may be lucky and either find a shorter algorithm or discover that the sequence of steps could fix other problems, too.

Now that we are somewhat familiar with our algorithm plan, time to see how it works in practice. First, we will explore procrastination and then overthinking, and find an optimal algorithm to solve both.

Chapter 6: The Procrastination Algorithm

How long would it take you to paint a 30x21 inch painting? Let's not get caught up in your artistic abilities, assume you are a practicing Bob Ross apprentice. So, what's your guesstimate? One month? Six months? One year, my perfectionistic friend? Whatever number popped up in your mind, you probably wouldn't have said 16 years. Because that's exactly how long Leonardo took da Vinci to paint the Mona Lisa.

Did da Vinci continuously dabble on his easel during this time? Nope. Why did it take him so long to finish our era's most famous portrait then? Well, he, like many of us, mere mortals, was affected by procrastination. And I would like to point out this guy was going places. Today we look at his work as the paragon of productivity and quality. He gave us The Last Supper, the

Vitruvian Man, and dozens of other world-famous paintings. But da Vinci was a curious and well-seasoned polymath. He left behind works on human anatomy, sketches of flying machines, and other "modern" (15th century modern) machinery and weaponry. And I would also like to add that many of his works were left unfinished.

Leonardo da Vinci was a productivity superstar. And excellent at procrastinating. Many of his unfinished projects are still considered beautiful, some for the very reason that they are unfinished. Quality work, even if it goes unfinished, is still worth your effort. So even if you fail to finish some of your projects, don't beat yourself up too harshly. Da Vinci did it, too.

Our greatest grievance with procrastination is not about finishing things. It's getting things started. There's something you need to do, but you can't make yourself do it. Despite how important the task is, you can't find the internal push to act. Familiar? We've all been there. The question is not, "do we procrastinate?" We all do that. The question is, how can we make optimal decisions on what to procrastinate on? What should we push to get started on? And most importantly, how?

What is procrastination anyway?

Procrastination is the classic pathology of time management. It is often swept under the same rug with laziness and avoidance. But these states of mind are not synonymous. Procrastination is the good solution of a bad mindset. When we are in an unproductive state of mind, say, we're afraid of something, procrastination can seem like a good idea to ease our fear. It's helpful to fix our momentary condition, but it doesn't help our long-term goals.

For example, we might fear the discomfort of adopting a new habit, like doing exercise regularly. Our mind boosts this perceived discomfort out of proportion. Our self-defense reflex will be triggered in response to this "threat." Our subconscious tells us just to stay put – if we don't act, no pain will come. Thus, the procrastination. Usually, we keep to this "solution" until the threat -and fear - of not doing the discomfort-causing activity becomes bigger than doing it. Say you went to the doctor who told you that you'll get a heart attack sooner than later if you don't lose weight. Having this new, bigger fear will prompt you into action.

Ideally, we don't want to wait until we get an unfavorable diagnosis, or an ultimatum at our job to stop procrastinating. Why do you think you're procrastinating on these things? Take a hard look. Can you become aware of exactly what thoughts are making you avoid the subject of your procrastination? Be vigilant to biases and possible negative conditioning when you answer these questions. Is it your opinion or has someone taught you to believe it? Sometimes the answer is as easy as allowing yourself to do something "badly". Or release some pressure off your shoulders. Remind yourself that it is okay to be afraid, and you will be fine regardless of the outcome.

Data Hunt

It's time to assess what you procrastinate on, how it makes you feel, and how it impacts your life.

Write a list of at least 10 things you usually procrastinate on. Yes, 10 because it's easy to write 3-5 examples of pretty much anything. After five examples, however, you need to exert actual cognitive effort to squeeze five more ideas. You will need to go deeper, think harder.

Ready? Go!

1.
2.
3.
4.
5.
6.
7.
8.
9.

10.

Once you have the 10 things you procrastinate on (hopefully, writing lists is not one of them), write about how they impact your life. For example, if you procrastinate on taking out the trash, its impact will be that your house will smell. Maybe it will attract a colony of fruit flies. It's uncomfortable, especially as fruit flies reproduce thousand-fold over two seconds, but it's not the worst thing you could ever imagine. But if you procrastinate on getting that stubborn pain in your stomach checked, you may end up in the hospital with pancreatitis. Please look at your procrastination list from above and now write their impact on your life. You can write just a few keywords for each. Or you can be descriptive and elaborate. It's up to you. You are not answering these questions for me. I'm just the annoying author who puts you to work. This exercise is for you. The answers you give result from deep introspection and self-reflection and will help improve your life. Also, they are essential to building our algorithm. So please, take some time to write about how your procrastination affects your life.

1.
2.
3.
4.
5.
6.
7.
8.
9.
10.

Done? If you hated this practice, I understand. I used to get annoyed at authors who asked me to write down this or that. I skipped these sections habitually. "I came here to read, not to write!" I protested. And for the longest time, I burnt my way through self-development books sharpening my reading skills only. One day, when Mercury was in retrograde, I gave in. "Fine," I thought, "I will complete these silly exercises as I read. Just to prove that they are useless." Ever since then, I have never read another self-help book *without* doing everything they requested me to do. You get a different level of experience and knowledge. Books such as this are not written solely to offer a pleasant read. If that's what you're seeking, pick up a fiction book or a biography. Books such as this help you get something more out of your reading than pure entertainment. You gain self-awareness, new self-management tools, or even new hope for better life quality. Enough pep talk. I trust you will do what's best for you.

The next section of self-reflection helps you explore how each procrastination item on your list affects your emotions? Do you feel anxiety, anger, restlessness, fear, stress? How much? Describe the feeling and the intensity of each.

    1.
    2.
    3.
    4.
    5.
    6.
    7.

8.

9.

10.

Now, based on everything you know, rank the first list (the one where you enumerated 10 things you procrastinate on) from 1-10, 10 being the worst. Worst, in this case, means that the subject of your procrastination has a very bad impact on your life, and it also causes you a lot of emotional suffering. The second and third lists can help to establish the order of the first list. You can check the life-impact and emotional-impact consequences for each procrastination subject.

If only machine learning was more advanced… it could do this computation in split seconds. But they can't think abstractly like this, so we need to make our assessments.

When you're done ranking the 10 items on your list, circle the top three things you procrastinate on, so nr. 10, 9, and 8.

Think about what would make things better for you? What may prompt you to take action in these instances? Can you think of a time when you overcame inaction? What did you do then? Whatever your answer is, the conclusion will be that any practice that soothes the emotions involved with that procrastination item (such as anxiety, fear, discomfort, or anger) will do the trick. Just think about these questions for now.

How do algorithms fit the picture?

We're almost at the part where we'll design our own life algorithms. But first, let's recap what algorithms are. An algorithm is a sequence of steps to perform a task given an initial situation. At their core, good algorithms have four simple characteristics:

Correct: The answer comes from previous knowledge and calculations and follows logic.

Efficient: The algorithm must use only the space and time that is necessary to get the best result.

Comprehensible: The algorithm can be understood by others.

Illustrative: The solution can create greater concepts, such as by sorting data. (Fisher, p. 7)[xxxviii]

We will create such algorithms to help us sort concepts and ideas into actionable steps.

Computer science helps us with providing algorithms for optimal stopping, scheduling our days, and predictions. But computers can't assess what the most important metrics are for us. If what mattered most to us was to find the best secretary candidate over an optimized amount of time, optimal stopping would work great. But in real life, you may have other concerns at hand. Things that the rule of 37% can't fix. For instance, you may care about hiring someone

who is great but is also in dire need of a job—
a single mom of three. Or you might want
someone who is a good secretary candidate
but could be groomed into another position.
You may care less about their capabilities and
more about what's the minimal money they
would work for.

With our life, we need to explore our
metrics and values first and create optimal,
repeatable strings of actions that lead us the
closest to our desires.

I chose two metrics we will measure
our procrastination against. One is the level of
stress it causes. The other is the level of
trouble it brings into our lives.

The Procrastination Algorithm

This is a list of how to build an algorithm in
the previous chapter.

1. "Step 1: Obtain a description of the
   problem. This step is much more
   difficult than it appears. ...
2. Step 2: Analyze the problem. ...

3. Step 3: Develop a base (base) algorithm. ...
4. Step 4: Refine the algorithm by adding more detail. ...
5. Step 5: Review the algorithm."[xxxix]

Write down item nr. 10 on your procrastination list.

Step 1: Obtain a description of the problem.

It's your responsibility to create a description of your problem. This can pose the most challenging part of the process. Why? Because you tend to be biased, have blind spots, and rely on unstated assumptions. Yet an accurate and complete problem detection is essential to design a good solution for it.

I procrastinated and stressed the most over my inability to sit down and write a book for almost a year.

Step 2: Analyze the problem.

In this step, we articulate the "starting and ending points for solving the problem. A good problem description makes it easier to perform this step."[xl]

My starting point is the inability to start writing. After days spent by me sitting down at the computer just to pop up immediately after and clean something in the house, the issue crystalized in my head. Due to Covid-19, I could work nowhere else but my house, a comfortable hub for procrastination. I simply can't work from home, and I had to realize.

My issue's starting point was easy to identify. But there are cases when identification is not that easy. When in trouble establishing the starting point, consider these questions:

- What information do I have available?[xli]

I have the information I can't get in a work mindset at home. I never could and never will.

- Where am I collecting this info from?

I'm collecting this data from my current self-observation and recalling my past behavior.

- What formulas pertain to the problem?

Isolation due to Covid-19. Being distracted easily by household tasks. Feeling weighed down by the negative mental health effects of the pandemic.

- What rules exist for working with this information?

Research has shown that relying on willpower and motivation is not smart. One needs to develop a set of routines to overcome inaction and commit to repeating them. Show up on the good days and the bad. This often starts with just committing to doing something for 5-10 minutes.

- What is the relationship between pieces of information?

Covid-19 forced coffee shops and coworking places to not accept customers indoors. This led to me needing to work from home. But I simply can't do quality work from there.

When trying to pin down the ending point, elaborate on the attributes of a solution. How does the ideal outcome look like? How will you know when the problem is solved? What steps could I commit to getting there? What am I willing/ unwilling to do?

- What new facts will I have once done?

I will know where and when I can be the most productive and motivated to get started.

- What changes will have been made?

Adoption of new, better habits that break down any resistance in my work moral.

- What things will no longer exist?

No more procrastination in my work life.

Step 3: Develop a base algorithm.

It's time to design a plan for solving the problem we're analyzing. Experts recommend starting with a base algorithm that focuses on a big part of the solution, and allows for details to be added later.

Problem: Low-productivity environment induced procrastination.

Base algorithm progress:

- Find a space where it's easy to get start way to get started.
- Find a way to maintain focus.
- Find a way to finish quality products.

I explored various "find a space and get started" strategies. I committed to sitting down at my computer in my backyard. This happened just before things opened again. I didn't allow myself to get off my computer until I sat there for 6 hours. I often just browsed the web. Was this a correct, efficient, comprehensible, and illustrative method? Comprehensible and illustrative, yes. But not efficient and certainly not correct. I had to tweak the components of this algorithm segment.

Web browsing was the obstacle, and I had to remove it. It wasn't hard. I installed an app called SelfControl that blocked out the intrusive sites. This solved one problem but generated another. I didn't browse the web anymore, but I noticed and worked on a lot of "urgent" yard work. I realized I need to get out of the house – the whole house, including the yard. By this point, coffee shops and other outdoor spaces were open.

I went to coffee shops with the timer and the self-control app. I was more productive, but the barista kept talking as he was bored for the lack of customers. Not good. Distracting. I had to tweak my algorithm further.

Finally, I landed in a coworking space.

I got to the perfect algorithm sequence that helped me get started and maintain my focus: - walk to the coworking space,
- settle in my cubicle,

- start the self-control app,
- set the timer for 6 hours.
- work.

This is an efficient, correct, comprehensible, and illustrative algorithm. It brings the same results each time I repeat this sequence of actions.

Step 4: Refine the algorithm by adding more details.

Once you get to this point, your work with the algorithm is almost done. Now you can add the details you weren't so focused on before. You can define:

- What time of the day are you the most productive to do your work?
- How many hours should you work?
- Do you prefer absolute silence or some focus music?
- Would you like to prime your mind before work with some yoga or meditation?

The number and depth of the details you add to your base algorithm are up to you and situation-dependent. You need to consider which details add something of value to your base algorithm and which are just another form of procrastination. If something is added to your sequence just to masquerade as productivity, it will not get you to your described solution. Similarly, it won't fit one of algorithms' main features, efficiency (the algorithm must use only the space and time absolutely necessary to get the best result). You also need to adapt the level of detail to your ability to process it consistently.

Allow time to incorporate the details in your algorithm. Think about every single detail you add to your base algorithm as an intermediate algorithm. Stop adding details when you see no improvement or the cost of improvement outweighs the benefits.

Step 5: Review the algorithm.

The final step is to review and track the algorithm. What should you look for? First, you need to see if the algorithm is easy to adopt in your life. And then track your performance over time using the algorithm and see if you are headed to solve your problem, in the short and long term.

Once you can confirm both aspects of the algorithm, congratulations! You just found a great algorithm that fits your lifestyle and solves your problem. But there is still one critical question to ask. Is this algorithm optimal? Can it be simplified? Can you automate some steps? Can you skip some? How can these changes affect performance? Can this solution be applied to another problem?

Exercise:

Now it is your turn. What worked for me in overcoming procrastination may not work for you. Design your algorithm to overcome your top 3 procrastination subjects.

Try something that you find helpful with your problem, tweak it. Add to it, subtract, test.

Repeat. Target the problematic variables with actionable step-sequences. Once something works, stick with it. Test its longevity. When the system is not producing the same results, add or take out a variable.

Chapter 7: The Overthinking Algorithm

Have you ever tossed and turned in your bed because you felt a little nod behind your ear or on your neck? To alleviate your worry, you googled what it could be. Based on your research, you concluded it is most likely a lymph node. You went back to bed with the assurance that you don't have terminal cancer when your eyes suddenly pop open again. You're such a worst-case scenario thinker! It's bad. Why should you think so negatively? What if you're doing yourself some intentional self-harm? Maybe you'll give yourself cancer with all the unnecessary cortisol you just pumped into your body. Twice. Thrice. Shoot. Maybe you should see a therapist? Okay, but what kind of therapist? Maybe you're hypochondriac and not negative? Then a psychiatrist would be a better option. Or would it? Who the hell knows. You google it. You feel bad about your incessant worry.

Maybe you have an anxiety disorder? No, you can't generalize your diagnosis just based on this one evening. Oh, no. What if you're in denial? Maybe this is what people with mental health problems do. They try to rationalize themselves out of it. Maybe you should just sleep on it, relax. But it's already 2 am! You realize you can only sleep 5 hours now. What if you'll be tired tomorrow...

On and on it goes...

The paragraph above is a classic example of overthinking. You take a piece of information and blow it out of proportion. Excessive thinking happens when your thought processes are out of control, injecting distress and anxiety into your life. Your brain's primary aim is to help you understand things more deeply and solve problems. But when it works overtime, be it in the shape of over-analyzing, over-judging, or over-controlling, it is unhelpful and inefficient.

We can overthink a lot of things, not just our health. We can get in a mental rabbit hole about life choices, from financial decisions to what to have for breakfast. We can add too many variables with too much data to our decision-making. For example, we can think about our breakfast as quick/ slow, and healthy/ with bacon. But when we want to find something quick, healthy, plus whole grain or fruits, plus filling or light, plus at home or takeout, plus... You get the point. The breakfast itself might be closer to the ideal with more complexity, but is it necessary, and in the end, will it be predictably better than something random that is just quick and healthy? Better predictions and outcomes are the reason we (over)think. Is this true?

The ability to think is the superpower of our species. It's normal to assume, the more we think, the better. That more thinking will lead us to better predictions and decisions. But this is not the case more often than you'd think. In machine learning, "researchers and statisticians call the problem - and question - of how hard to think and how many factors to consider "overfitting."[xlii] There is wisdom in deliberately thinking less. Applying overfitting in your life can help you diminish the mental fatigue overthinking generates. You can optimize your life to "think just the right amount and depth."[xliii]

Why stop overthinking?

In mild doses overthinking is not a problem. It's a part of the human condition, and sometimes it can help you get better results, find more accurate solutions. But if it becomes chronic and it interferes with your ability to function in your life, that's a problem. According to therapist Danielle Syslo, overthinking is usually caused by stress or anxiety. Maintaining either state for long can be detrimental not only to your day's quality but also long-term health. Overthinking can seriously impact your mental health and leads to emotional distress. Some people adopt unhealthy coping strategies such as substance abuse or overeating to escape this state of mental misery.[xliv]

Chronic overthinking can be the harbinger of underlying anxiety or stress issues. If that's the case, this book won't offer sufficient support as the scope of this chapter is to alleviate the symptoms (overthinking) of these deeper problems. Talk to your primary care doctor or therapist to identify if you have chronic stress or anxiety problems.

Explore your overthinking pathways.

First notice your overthinking patterns. What triggers them; what people, emotions, or life events? Do you overthink your health, financial plans, self-worth, or work? Do you have perfectionist tendencies? Do you ruminate a lot about the injustices of the world in general? Take inventory of the key aspects of your overthinking problem. But hey, don't overthink it.

Write down 10 things that you ruminate, perfect, overthink the most. Just like you did it in the previous chapter, jot down the 10 most relevant subjects you tend to overthink. Be specific. Don't just write "my health". Write down the specific health issue you ruminate on. For example, I fear I have cancer every time I find an inflated lymph node. Or I fear I'm developing dementia every time I forget something I know I should know. It can easily happen that half of your rumination list will be health-related. Or money-related. Or relationship related. It's okay. It will show you what your current fears in life are.

1.
2.
3.
4.
5.
6.
7.
8.
9.
10.

Done? Good. Look at your list. Is there a dominating life aspect occupying most of your (over)thinking? Do you find this revelation surprising or you knew you tend to overthink that life aspect?

Now, go through your list and write a few words on how the specific overthinking subject affects your life. Do you stay in a foul mood for days or do you snap out of it in a few minutes? Overthinking what to have for dinner usually produces less distress than a three-hour Google-doctor consultation about your numb pinky toe. Some folks can spend a lot of money to investigate all their worries. Others can't help but talk to their loved ones about it. Write about your overthinking experience, collect data.

1.
2.
3.
4.
5.
6.
7.
8.

9.

10.

When you're done with this task, reflect on how you feel after these overthinking "sessions?" Are you stressed, worried, exhausted, etc.? Write about your emotional experience.

1.

2.

3.

4.

5.

6.

7.

8.

9.

10.

Time to rank your overthinking subjects. Which causes the most distress or stalemate in your life? Rank the 10 things from 1-10, 10 being the worst.

The overthinking algorithm.

Optimizing your overthinking will depend on the gap between what you can measure and what matters to you. If you have access to error-free facts on a subject that matters a great deal to you, sure, think long and hard about it. Subjects such as this are rare. More commonly, we have limited, inaccurate, and error-prone data floating in high uncertainty. Stopping rumination early does us a great service. If you don't have clarity on the metrics your college application will be evaluated on, and by whom, it is not productive to add the extra time to make it perfect according to your guess at what perfection may mean to the evaluators. More uncertainty creates a bigger gap between what you can know and measure and reality. So overthinking these scenarios brings about only diminishing returns. In these cases, prioritize simplicity and stop early. "The upshot of early stopping is that sometimes it's not a matter of choosing between being rational and going with our first instinct. Going with our first instinct can be the rational choice. The more complex, unstable, and uncertain the decision, the more rational an approach that is."[Algorithms to Live By,] [xlv]

Let's recall the list for how to build an algorithm.

1. "Step 1: Obtain a description of the problem.
2. Step 2: Analyze the problem.
3. Step 3: Develop a base algorithm.
4. Step 4: Refine the algorithm by adding more detail.
5. Step 5: Review the algorithm."[xlvi]

Write down item nr. 10 on your overthinking list. Before we proceed, let's consider item nr. 10. Is this a subject worthy of more complex and longer thinking? Answer these questions. Do high levels of certainty surround this subject? Do I have sufficient, error-free, relevant data on this subject? If you responded yes to both questions, then this specific subject might benefit from more complex thinking. If so, skip this one and write down subject nr. 9 on your overthinking list. Don't run the "certainty – error-free data" question combo on this one. Start by solving nr. 10 with complex thinking first. Until nr. 10 is unresolved, there is no need to overthink another subject (such as nr.9) simultaneously. If you responded no to one or both of the "certainty-error-free data" questions, work on subject nr. 10 from your overthinking list.

Step 1: Obtain a description of the problem.

Item nr. 10 on my overthinking list is my utility and contribution to my family as a husband and father. I often feel I should do more, earn more, be more present. You get my point. My wife and children never complained about me not being an adequate breadwinner or devoted father. It's all in my head. Therefore, I have insufficient flawed data to support the "I am a bad husband and dad" thesis. Also, the certainty of me being such a person is low. My biggest overthinking struggle, thus, is a perfect candidate for this exercise. Ruminating over this subject is unproductive, harmful, and anxiety-provoking. It needs to go.

Problem: I ruminate a lot about being a bad husband and father.

Step 2: Analyze the problem.

Remember, this step aims to determine both the starting and ending points for solving this problem.[xlvii]

Let's find the starting point by answering these questions:

- What data are available?

The available data contradicts my beliefs. Our bills are paid in time. Our fridge is never empty. My family members reassured me that I am a great husband and father.

- Where is that data?

Some of the data is factual – bills and paychecks are numerical, quantitative. Other aspects of the data are qualitative, like my inner state, my wife's and kids' emotions.

- What formulas pertain to the problem?

For the income part, a simple formula would be: as long as you make more than you spend, you won't bankrupt your family. Keep a budget, track your income and expenses, and see where you stand.

For subjective assessments such as your wife's opinion of how good a husband you are, it's sufficient to trust in what she says. Your wife must know you well, and it's not in her interest to lie to you. The fact that your kids, other people who know you closely, reinforce what she said, is a bonus.

- What rules exist for working with the data?

It's hard to pinpoint rules for such subjective matters. But some ideas to consider are: don't try to solve this problem when you're in a negative mindset. Wait until you're calm and neutral about the issue. Trying to put out fires in the moment can lead to rushed algorithm creation that is not sustainable, and it would further erode your self-esteem and make you overthink things more.

- What relationships exist among the data values?

The small depressive episode linked to procrastination and reduced work output can give a lot of room for overthinking. The fact that I still provide well to my family is linked with their reported satisfaction.

Now that we know where we stand, let's see where we want to get. We will explore questions to determine our end point:

- What new facts will we have?

We will gather more information on our overthinking pattern, worst-case scenario thinking, and see how many of these support the subject of our overthinking (i.e. "I'm a bad father, husband."). The more information will disapprove what we ruminate on, the safer we will feel to let that idea go.

If more data will confirm our fears in our overthinking, despair not. If what you ruminate on is true, now you'll have more knowledge on the subject, and you can create a more efficient strategy to tackle the problem. For example, you have a bad upper belly pain and you investigate what it could be after a long session of overthinking. You are also experiencing bloating and have heartburn. Based on your research, these symptoms could indicate that you're developing an ulcer. The extra information helped you zoom on a potentially dangerous health condition. You can take targeted action, avoid acidic food, and visit your primary care doctor or the emergency room, depending on the severity of your pain.

-   What items will have changed?

The goal of the overthinking algorithm is to alleviate the distress that causes racing thoughts. After you perform the sequential steps to ease your mind, you'd get to a place where you can let go of overthinking, or you can engage in a more targeted solution. Worrying and overthinking solved no problem. Calm, targeted action did. `

- What changes will have been made to those items?

The changes applied to overthinking are mindfulness and intentionality. You learn to notice and catch yourself when you're spiraling into overthinking and decide not to go down the usual rabbit hole. You will ask targeted questions instead and gather data.

- What things will no longer exist?

While overthinking won't disappear completely from your life, you will have a shifted perspective on it. You can grasp when you're in the overthinking spiral and stop or reframe the thoughts before they make you feel miserable. It's one thing to ruminate for a bit. But believing and accepting these thoughts as the truth and suffering for it is a different story.

Step 3: Develop a base algorithm.

It's time to design a plan for solving your overthinking problem. Again, let's start with a base algorithm that focuses on a big part of the solution. We can add details later.

Base algorithm progress in overcoming overthinking:

1. Learn to catch yourself in the moment you're spiraling into overthinking. (Self-awareness.)
2. Understand the hidden reasons for your overthinking. (Self-knowledge.)
3. Investigate the accuracy and validity of your thoughts, gather data.
4. Based on the data, you can discover that:
    a. Your fear that leads to overthinking is unwarranted. You consciously reframe your thoughts to reflect reality and gently let go of the subject of your rumination.
    b. Your fear that leads to overthinking is warranted. You narrow down on the problem that you proved to be real, and leave overthinking out of the picture.
5. Solutions.

a. You practice journaling, meditation, yoga, jogging, or any other self-soothing activity that allows you to calm your overthinking mind. (Point 4. a.)
b. You build an algorithm to solve the real root problem that you identified in point 4. b.

Step 4: Refine the algorithm by adding more detail.

You're almost there. Your algorithm still needs some tweaks, though. Now you can add the details you weren't so focused on before. You can define:

- How can you catch yourself when you're about to overthink something? Try out these tips to identify the best way you can catch your overthinking. Is it easier to notice changing sensations in your body? For example, if your chest tightens and you become nervous when you overthink, you can anchor these sensations for identification. If your brain empties and you suddenly feel a lack of energy, that could be your cue. The more aware you become of how your body reacts to overthinking, the easier it will get to catch it early.

- What tools will you use to understand your reasons for overthinking and test your thoughts' validity? These two steps call for data gathering. But how? Will you journal? Or do you prefer asking people? Do you want to look up studies, statistics, more tangible data? Depending on your overthinking, get creative on how you gather information. My example is related to myself; it's of emotional nature. Collecting factual, measurable information is more challenging. If my problem was directed to my weight, it would be easier to look up plain numbers for ideal BMI (body mass index) and other aspects of healthy living.

- What self-soothing activity is the best fit for you to practice mitigating the urge to overthink? You will need to experiment with different methods and see what works. If you find something that helps you tame your overthinking, use it the next time, too. If it still works, you may have found a winner.

You get to decide the depth of the details you add to your base algorithm. Different overthinking subjects may also call for different details. The algorithm's core is the same (points 1-5), but you need to consider which details are adding something of value to your solution. If something gets added to your sequence for no good reason, it may not get you to your described end solution. Or, if it does, it won't fit one of algorithms' main features, efficiency (the algorithm must use only the space and time necessary to get the best result).

Allow time to incorporate the details in your algorithm. Think about every single detail you add to your base algorithm as an intermediate algorithm. Stop adding details when you see no improvement or the cost of improvement outweighs the benefits.

Step 5: Review the algorithm.

There is nothing left but to review and track the algorithm. Check if the algorithm is easy to adopt in your life. Track your performance over time using the algorithm and see if you are headed to solve your overthinking problem, in the short and long term.

Don't forget to optimize the algorithm. Simplify it if you can. Skip steps or details if they prove to be unnecessary.

Exercise:

In this chapter, we talked about overthinking, and I shared with you the five steps I tackle overthinking. Now it is your turn to design your sequence to find a solution. What worked for me may not work for you. Design your own algorithm to overcome your top 3 overthinking subjects.

Conclusion

We, humans, are not machines. But this doesn't mean we shouldn't try to adopt some best practices machines use. Stubborn problems in our lives may benefit from us thinking about solutions in terms of algorithms.

Algorithms take decision fatigue out of our daily lives. Just like we learned that the ideal day starts by washing our face, brushing our teeth, and having breakfast, we can learn problem-solving sequences the same way. We don't think about our morning routine, we just do it. Ideally, we'll get to a point where we don't think about overthinking, we just perform the algorithm.

The good thing about this algorithmic thinking is that you can apply it to any problem. In this book, I presented you with a tangible, easy-to-detect and follow problem like procrastinating on work. I also showed that you could use this algorithm to a more abstract, emotionally charged issue such as overthinking your self-worth.

We are not machines, I repeat. The goal of this book is not to push you to monotonize and automatize every aspect of your life and perform a set sequence of steps to deal with every issue you face. The goal is to have a good tool to consistently overcome one or two major problems you struggle with the most.

It's up to you to adopt as much or as little from this book as you need.

Good luck.

A. R.

Summary Guide

Chapter 1: Homo Irrationalis

- Our rationality has been tainted by our feelings where the two are impossible to extricate.

- We've developed these shortcuts, known as "heuristics," as a survival mechanism that enables us to act more efficiently during a life-or-death situation. But, as we've evolved, it has become a less beneficial part of our everyday lives.

- Our brains don't just do this to make us happy; they do it to save energy. We only have so much brain power to give to decision making every day, so we have to make sure that we save it for the important stuff.

- Our brain prefers and therefore seeks easier comparisons and calculations.

- Often, when we believe we're being logical and basing our choices on facts, we're just using our memories and biases to conclude.

- Emotional thinking comes to us naturally while rational decision making is learned.

- To make sure that we're taking both aspects of thinking into account and start making rational thinking the norm rather than the exception, we can produce and use formulas for thinking and decision making to replace those we have that rely on biases and shortcuts.

Chapter 2: Machina Sapiens

- Algorithms are always learning and evolving based on the information we give them. The more we search and use them, the better they become at knowing what we like and want.

- An algorithm decides what to show you or produce, while machine learning is a subfield of AI that tracks your online presence and interactions to understand your tendencies and habits.

- An algorithm is merely a sequence of steps to perform a task given an initial situation.

- Good algorithms have four simple characteristics: correct, efficient, comprehensible, illustrative.

- We, humans, have something machines and AI don't. We can solve problems using emotions, abstraction, and imagination.

- If we put the rational side of algorithms *and* our abilities of imagination and abstraction together, we can achieve incredible things.

Chapter 3: Where Machines Teach Humans

- 37% is the tipping point between having seen enough of what's out there to make an informed decision and passing by so many options you limit yourself.

- While optimal stopping is about ensuring data is gathered, the threshold rule is about leveraging the information we *already have* as efficiently as possible.

Chapter 4: Predictions, Dopamine, Machines, And Humans

- Dopamine as the brain's happy chemical, but it does a lot more than put us in a good mood. Dopamine is the communicator neuron, the SMS of brain cells.

- Dopamine was more concerned with predicting good results than actually receiving rewards, and the chemicals were seen anew as "prediction neurons."

- In life-threatening situation, the signal to the hypothalamus is often faster than that to our thalamus, causing us to have bodily reactions before our thoughts can catch up.

- Bayes' theorem suggests that we should use any evidence we gain to update and verify our hypothesis. This algorithm uses the basic principle of cause and effect and the power of mathematics to assess the probability of an event given the situation and prior outcomes.

Chapter 5: Diy Algorithm Design

- No matter how big or small our troubles are, their solution always starts with a plan. In this book, we call that plan an algorithm.

- Five key steps to create our algorithm:

  - "Step 1: Obtain a description of the problem.

  - Step 2: Analyze the problem.

  - Step 3: Develop a base algorithm.

  - Step 4: Refine the algorithm by adding more detail.

  - Step 5: Review the algorithm."[xlviii]

Chapter 6: The Procrastination Algorithm

- Our greatest grievance with procrastination is not about finishing things. It's getting things started.

- Once you have the 10 things you procrastinate on (hopefully, writing lists is not one of them), write about how they impact your life.

- The next section of self-reflection helps you explore how each procrastination item on your list affects your emotions.

Chapter 7: The Overthinking Algorithm

- Excessive thinking happens when your thought processes are out of control, injecting distress and anxiety into your life.
- Chronic overthinking can be the harbinger of underlying anxiety or stress issues.

- First notice your overthinking patterns. What triggers them; what people, emotions, or life events?

- Write down 10 things that you ruminate, perfect, overthink the most.

Before You Go…

I would be so very grateful if you would take a few seconds and rate or review this book on Amazon! Reviews – testimonials of your experience - are critical to an author's livelihood. While reviews are surprisingly hard to come by, they provide the life blood for me being able to stay in business and dedicate myself to the thing I love the most, writing.

If this book helped, touched, or spoke to you in any way, please leave me a review and give me your honest feedback.

Thank you so much for reading this book! Don't forget to claim your free gift:

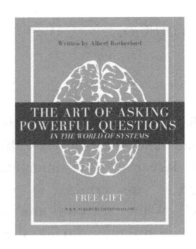

Visit www.albertrutherford.com and download your FREE GIFT: The Art of Asking Powerful Questions in the World of Systems

References

Ariely, D. (2009). *Predictably Irrational.* HarperCollins.

Big Think. (2021, July 20). *The Science of 'Herd Mentality'.* https://bigthink.com/singleton/the-science-of-herd-mentality.

Christian, B., & Griffiths, T. (2016). *Algorithms to Live by: The Computer Science of Human Decisions.* William Collins.

Domingos, P. (2015). *The Master Algorithm: How the Quest for the Ultimate Learning Machine Will Remake our World.* Basic Books.

Edwards, S., Dorn, B., & Sanders, D. (2012). Problem Solving and Algorithms. Objects First. http://sofia.cs.vt.edu/cs1114-ebooklet/chapter4.html

Fisher, D. H. (2019, January 16). *Algorithms in Everyday Life.* Vanderbilt.

https://www.vanderbilt.edu/olli/class-materials/InnovativeThinkingSession1.pdf

Lehrer, J. (2009). *How We Decide.* Houghton Mifflin Harcourt.

McLeod, S. (2019, December 28). *Solomon Asch- Conformity Experiment.* Simply Psychology. https://www.simplypsychology.org/asch-conformity.html.

Morgan, A. (2019, October 10). *Even If You Think You're Logical You're Not.* Medium. https://medium.com/the-creative-machine/even-if-you-think-youre-logical-you-re-not-33030adf15b1.

Morin, A. (2016, February 12). 6 Tips to Stop Overthinking. Psychology Today. https://www.psychologytoday.com/us/blog/what-mentally-strong-people-dont-do/201602/6-tips-stop-overthinking

Wilson, R. (Narrator), Lukyanova, T. (Producer), & Gordon, C. (Executive Producer). (2021). Chess (Season 3, Episode 6) [TV Series Episode]. In E. Klein & J. Posner (Creators), *Explained.* VoxMedia.

Endnotes

[i] Ariely, D. (2009). Predictably Irrational. HarperCollins.
[ii] Morgan, A. (2019, October 10). Even If You Think You're Logical You're Not. Medium. https://medium.com/the-creative-machine/even-if-you-think-youre-logical-you-re-not-33030adf15b1.
[iii] Ariely, D. (2009). Predictably Irrational. HarperCollins.
[iv] Ariely, D. (2009). Predictably Irrational. HarperCollins.
[v] Big Think. (2021, July 20). The Science of 'Herd Mentality'. https://bigthink.com/singleton/the-science-of-herd-mentality.
[vi] McLeod, S. (2019, December 28). Solomon Asch-Conformity Experiment. Simply Psychology. https://www.simplypsychology.org/asch-conformity.html.
[vii] Big Think. (2021, July 20). The Science of 'Herd Mentality'. https://bigthink.com/singleton/the-science-of-herd-mentality.
[viii] Fisher, D. H. (2019, January 16). Algorithms in Everyday Life. Vanderbilt. https://www.vanderbilt.edu/olli/class-materials/InnovativeThinkingSession1.pdf
[ix] Fisher, D. H. (2019, January 16). Algorithms in Everyday Life. Vanderbilt. https://www.vanderbilt.edu/olli/class-materials/InnovativeThinkingSession1.pdf
[x] Christian, B., & Griffiths, T. (2016). Algorithms to Live by: The Computer Science of Human Decisions. William Collins.
[xi] Christian, B., & Griffiths, T. (2016). Algorithms to Live by: The Computer Science of Human Decisions. William

Collins.

[xii] Christian, B., & Griffiths, T. (2016). Algorithms to Live by: The Computer Science of Human Decisions. William Collins.

[xiii] Christian, B., & Griffiths, T. (2016). Algorithms to Live by: The Computer Science of Human Decisions. William Collins.

[xiv] Christian, B., & Griffiths, T. (2016). Algorithms to Live by: The Computer Science of Human Decisions. William Collins.

[xv] Christian, B., & Griffiths, T. (2016). Algorithms to Live by: The Computer Science of Human Decisions. William Collins.

[xvi] Christian, B., & Griffiths, T. (2016). Algorithms to Live by: The Computer Science of Human Decisions. William Collins.

[xvii] Christian, B., & Griffiths, T. (2016). Algorithms to Live by: The Computer Science of Human Decisions. William Collins.

[xviii] Christian, B., & Griffiths, T. (2016). Algorithms to Live by: The Computer Science of Human Decisions. William Collins.

[xix] Christian, B., & Griffiths, T. (2016). Algorithms to Live by: The Computer Science of Human Decisions. William Collins.

[xx] Christian, B., & Griffiths, T. (2016). Algorithms to Live by: The Computer Science of Human Decisions. William Collins.

[xxi] Christian, B., & Griffiths, T. (2016). Algorithms to Live by: The Computer Science of Human Decisions. William Collins.

[xxii] Lehrer, J. (2009). How We Decide. Houghton Mifflin Harcourt.

[xxiii] Lehrer, J. (2009). How We Decide. Houghton Mifflin Harcourt.

[xxiv] Lehrer, J. (2009). How We Decide. Houghton Mifflin Harcourt.

[xxv] Lehrer, J. (2009). How We Decide. Houghton Mifflin

Harcourt.

[xxvi] Lehrer, J. (2009). How We Decide. Houghton Mifflin Harcourt.

[xxvii] Lehrer, J. (2009). How We Decide. Houghton Mifflin Harcourt.

[xxviii] Lehrer, J. (2009). How We Decide. Houghton Mifflin Harcourt.

[xxix] Domingos, P. (2015). The Master Algorithm: How the Quest for the Ultimate Learning Machine Will Remake our World. Basic Books.

[xxx] Domingos, P. (2015). The Master Algorithm: How the Quest for the Ultimate Learning Machine Will Remake our World. Basic Books.

[xxxi] Domingos, P. (2015). The Master Algorithm: How the Quest for the Ultimate Learning Machine Will Remake our World. Basic Books.

[xxxii] Domingos, P. (2015). The Master Algorithm: How the Quest for the Ultimate Learning Machine Will Remake our World. Basic Books.

[xxxiii] Domingos, P. (2015). The Master Algorithm: How the Quest for the Ultimate Learning Machine Will Remake our World. Basic Books.

[xxxiv] Edwards, S., Dorn, B., & Sanders, D. (2012). Problem Solving and Algorithms. Objects First. http://sofia.cs.vt.edu/cs1114-ebooklet/chapter4.html

[xxxv] Edwards, S., Dorn, B., & Sanders, D. (2012). Problem Solving and Algorithms. Objects First. http://sofia.cs.vt.edu/cs1114-ebooklet/chapter4.html

[xxxvi] Edwards, S., Dorn, B., & Sanders, D. (2012). Problem Solving and Algorithms. Objects First. http://sofia.cs.vt.edu/cs1114-ebooklet/chapter4.html

[xxxvii] Edwards, S., Dorn, B., & Sanders, D. (2012). Problem Solving and Algorithms. Objects First. http://sofia.cs.vt.edu/cs1114-ebooklet/chapter4.html

[xxxviii] Fisher, D. H. (2019, January 16). Algorithms in Everyday Life. Vanderbilt. https://www.vanderbilt.edu/olli/class-materials/InnovativeThinkingSession1.pdf

[xxxix] Edwards, S., Dorn, B., & Sanders, D. (2012). Problem Solving and Algorithms. Objects First. http://sofia.cs.vt.edu/cs1114-ebooklet/chapter4.html

[xl] Edwards, S., Dorn, B., & Sanders, D. (2012). Problem Solving and Algorithms. Objects First. http://sofia.cs.vt.edu/cs1114-ebooklet/chapter4.html

[xl] Edwards, S., Dorn, B., & Sanders, D. (2012). Problem Solving and Algorithms. Objects First. http://sofia.cs.vt.edu/cs1114-ebooklet/chapter4.html

[xli] Edwards, S., Dorn, B., & Sanders, D. (2012). Problem Solving and Algorithms. Objects First. http://sofia.cs.vt.edu/cs1114-ebooklet/chapter4.html

[xlii] Christian, B., & Griffiths, T. (2016). Algorithms to Live by: The Computer Science of Human Decisions. William Collins.

[xliii] Christian, B., & Griffiths, T. (2016). Algorithms to Live by: The Computer Science of Human Decisions. William Collins.

[xliv] Morin, A. (2016, February 12). 6 Tips to Stop Overthinking. Psychology Today. https://www.psychologytoday.com/us/blog/what-mentally-strong-people-dont-do/201602/6-tips-stop-overthinking

[xlv] Christian, B., & Griffiths, T. (2016). Algorithms to Live by: The Computer Science of Human Decisions. William Collins.

[xlvi] Edwards, S., Dorn, B., & Sanders, D. (2012). Problem Solving and Algorithms. Objects First. http://sofia.cs.vt.edu/cs1114-ebooklet/chapter4.html

[xlvii] Edwards, S., Dorn, B., & Sanders, D. (2012). Problem Solving and Algorithms. Objects First. http://sofia.cs.vt.edu/cs1114-ebooklet/chapter4.html

[xlviii] Edwards, S., Dorn, B., & Sanders, D. (2012). Problem Solving and Algorithms. Objects First. http://sofia.cs.vt.edu/cs1114-ebooklet/chapter4.html